W9-AYO-201

Date Due

FEB 1 8 1997			

PETER ILYICH
TCHAIKOVSKY

Richard Tames

Franklin Watts

New York ● London ● Toronto ● Sydney

Contents

© Franklin Watts 1991

Franklin Watts, Inc.
387 Park Avenue South
New York, N.Y. 10016

Phototypeset by: JB Type, Hove, East Sussex
Printed in: Belgium
Series Editor: Hazel Poole
Designed by: Nick Cannan

Library of Congress Cataloging-in-Publication Data
Tames, Richard.
    Peter Ilyich Tchaikovsky/Richard Tames.
        p.   cm. — (Lifetimes)
    Includes index.
    Summary: Examines Tchaikovsky's life and musical achievements in
the context of his historical period.
    ISBN 0-531-14108-X
    1. Tchaikovsky, Peter Ilyich, 1840-1893 — Juvenile literature.
2. Composers — Soviet Union — Biography — Juvenile literature.
[1. Tchaikovsky, Peter Ilyich, 1840-1893. 2. Composers.] I. Title.
II. Series: Tames, Richard. Lifetimes.
ML 3930.C4T3   1991
780'.92 – dc20
[B]
[92]   90-38304
                                                           CIP
                                                      AC MN

An Uncertain Beginning

"If it had not been for music I should have gone mad," Tchaikovsky once wrote. His passionate, dramatic compositions seem to confirm this. Outwardly his life was largely uneventful. For most of it he lived comfortably and, in the end, gained wealth and success. But the man within was a soul in torment. So shy that he shrank even from private parties, he was terrified of the concert platform. A prey to irrational terrors, he once conducted with one hand only, the other being propped under his chin to stop his head from shaking so badly.

These emotional problems were made worse by his confused sexuality. It is now clear that Tchaikovsky was attracted to men rather than women. But in 19th century Russia, homosexuality was regarded with horror. Even the most sympathetic people would have thought of it as a condition requiring medical treatment. So Tchaikovsky also had to live with the fear of a scandal that would disgrace his whole family. And there remained the constant pressure to pursue "normal" relationships with women. These were to push him into encounters that were awkward at best and in one case quite disastrous.

It is, therefore, perhaps ironic that this troubled and unhappy man should have produced melodies of sweeping power and haunting sweetness, which are recognized as some of the world's best-loved **"Romantic"** music. For Tchaikovsky's own life was a romance unfulfilled.

Tchaikovsky was born on May 7, 1840, at Kamsko-Votinsk, Russia, in the province of Viatka, west of the Ural mountains, where his father was a mines' inspector. He was christened Pyotr (Peter) and given the second name Ilyitch (son of Ilia) from his father's first name, according to Russian custom. Peter was the second son. The eldest, Nikolai (Nicholas), was named after the reigning Tsar, Nicholas I. In order after Peter came Ippolit (Hippolyte), Alexandra (Sasha), his favorite sister, and the twins, Anatol and Modeste. Modeste, who was also a homosexual, was especially close to him and was to publish an edition of the composer's letters after his death.

Peter's mother, Alexandra Andreievna, came from an old French family. A dutiful wife, she was also a cultured person who could speak French and German and play the piano and sing. But these were drawing-room accomplishments and her talents were no greater than those of many well-to-do women of the day. Unlike his hero Mozart, Tchaikovsky did not have the headstart of being brought up in a musical family.

Nor did he have a secure and settled childhood. His parents were

rather distant with him, so he became very fond of his young French governess, Fanny Dürbach. She taught him to speak French and German, which he learned to do well. But when the family moved to Moscow in 1848, Fanny was not taken with them and Peter was very upset. Soon afterward they moved again to St. Petersburg,

The country house where Tchaikovsky was born and spent his earliest years.

where the bewildered child caught measles so badly that he nearly died. Then suddenly they were off again to the Urals, where his father had found a new job, managing a foundry.

Peter began to play the piano while he was still a small child. His first teacher was Maria Markovna Palchikova, a freed **serf**. Within a year he could play better than she could. The little boy was fascinated by the family's "Orchestrion," a sort of over-sized musical box which played tunes mechanically. It was hearing tunes from the opera *Don Giovanni* on the Orchestrion that gave Peter his lifelong admiration for their composer, Mozart, and that, in turn, decided his future. "It was due to Mozart that I devoted my life to music," he wrote many years later. But no one suspected when he was a child that one day he would become a famous composer.

At the age of 10, young Peter was sent back to St. Petersburg to study and prepare for enrollment in the School of Jurisprudence. This would lead him on to a career in the Ministry of Justice. His father, like most of the Russian nobility, had been a state official. And this would be the future for the son. Too "nervous" to follow his father as an engineer, he would become a legal expert. But Peter's first experience of legal training got off to a very bad start when an outbreak of **scarlet fever** closed the school soon after he arrived. He was packed off to stay with friends of

Tchaikovsky's father, flanked by two of his sons. Prepared to encourage Peter's music, he was advised against it.

the family and while he was with them, their son died of the killer disease. Tchaikovsky felt guilty for years afterward, fearing that he had brought the infection with him.

Peter was a reluctant scholar, who worked without interest, but he was naturally bright and passed into the school's upper division without too much of a problem. Meanwhile he kept up his interest in music and took lessons from Rudolf Kündinger, a well-known concert pianist. Kündinger was impressed by the boy's ability to **improvise**, but beyond that thought he had no unusual talent. When Peter's father asked the teacher if he should change his mind and consider encouraging the boy's interest in the piano with a view to a career, Kündinger advised him against it. He had, he later admitted, "no real faith in Peter Ilyitch's gift for music."

Peter's personal life continued to be dogged by tragedy. When he was 14, his mother caught **cholera** and died. He was heartbroken for, despite her coldness, he had adored her.

At the age of 19, the young Tchaikovsky entered the Ministry of Justice in St. Petersburg as a First Class Clerk. He remained there for four years, bored but dutiful. A famous story tells of him absent-mindedly tearing an official document into strips, rolling them into pellets and swallowing them, so eating the whole thing. But at least his duties were not heavy

Mozart (1756-91), the musical genius who was Tchaikovsky's lifelong hero.

ones. He was able to take a leave of three months to accompany a relative around Europe, acting as his interpreter. And he had plenty of time for music. He played the piano and went to concerts. He joined the Ministry's own choral group, and in 1861, he began to study musical theory under Nikolai Zaremba, the Head of the Russian Musical Society, which was to become a formal Conservatory or music academy in 1862.

One of Tchaikovsky's other teachers was the composer and pianist Anton Rubinstein, who became the first Director of the St.

Petersburg Conservatory. Correcting the young man's exercises, Rubinstein saw real signs of talent but had to criticize his pupil for careless work. Tchaikovsky began to realize that he had to be serious about his music in order to make real progress. When he failed to get a promotion he had wanted at the Ministry, he decided to resign and start his career all over again. Entering the Conservatory at 22 years old, he was older than most of the other students. But he also had more experience and at least he could support himself by teaching pupils of his own. He lived simply

A scene from Mozart's *Don Giovanni*. Tchaikovsky's operas met mixed success.

and worked hard. He learned the organ and mastered the flute, which he then played in the Conservatory orchestra.

As a young government official, Tchaikovsky had disliked his work but appeared to enjoy his social life, going to the theater and opera, dressing fashionably and generally making the most of living in a great capital city. As a music student he was doing something he loved, but could no longer afford to indulge himself. And he was learning the pain of having his own music criticized. This was to be a problem for him throughout his life, although it didn't stop him from having very strong opinions about other people's music.

In 1864, Rubinstein was very critical of one of Tchaikovsky's early compositions *The Storm Overture*. Tchaikovsky then had to prepare his graduation piece. Rubinstein ordered him to devise a new setting of the *Ode to Joy*, a poem by the German writer Schiller, which Beethoven had used for the famous last movement of his great Ninth symphony. Tchaikovsky disliked Beethoven's music but completed the task. He was, however, too shy to appear at the graduation concert where his piece was performed. Rubinstein was furious with him for being absent. But he still allowed him to graduate — and awarded him the silver medal.

(Below) **St. Petersburg, Russia's capital and "window on the west."** (Right) **Opera-goers returning from a gala performance.**

"The Five"

In the 18th century, most educated Europeans accepted the idea of a common culture. They spoke French as an international language, read the classics of ancient Rome and put up buildings in the style of ancient Greece. The French Revolution in politics and the "Romantic" movement in culture provoked a new concern for national differences in language and the arts. In the new age of nationalism, music was seen as a particularly strong way of expressing the "soul" of a people and there was a great revival of interest in folk tunes as an inspiration for classical composers.

In Russia, the leader of the nationalist revival was Mikhail Glinka. His followers — Balakirev, Rimsky-Korsakov, César Cui, Borodin and Mussorgsky — became known as "The Five." They did not accept Tchaikovsky as one of their number because they disapproved of the influence on him of the German-trained Rubinstein. Despite this, Tchaikovsky admired some of their work (though not Borodin or Mussorgsky's) and was strongly influenced by Balakirev in two of his most memorable compositions, the *Romeo and Juliet* overture and the *Manfred* symphony. He also, in approved nationalist style, made use of peasant tunes in his own works. His first string quartet incorporated a song he heard a carpenter singing outside his room at his sister's house in the country. His second symphony, known as the *Little Russian*, was based on common themes of folk music. Perhaps, ironically, Tchaikovsky was to win far more renown for Russian music abroad than any of the nationalists.

Mikhail Glinka (1804-57), leader of the revival of a Russian national style in music, and inspirer of "the Five."

Years of Struggle

Even before he graduated from the St. Petersburg Conservatory, Tchaikovsky had been offered (thanks to Anton Rubinstein) a job as professor of harmony at the newly-established Moscow Conservatory, where the director was Rubinstein's younger brother, Nikolai. Now the nervous young Tchaikovsky had to face classes of students as their teacher. He tried to cope by working them and himself very hard — and by drinking heavily. This was to be a lifelong refuge and not at all uncommon among the Russian upper classes. He excused it in himself by pleading that "For me, a man harassed with nerves, it is simply impossible to live without the poison of alcohol."

Tchaikovsky also had problems with his new employer. Although his salary was small, Nikolai Rubinstein insisted that he spend most of his first month's pay on some decent clothes because he looked so shabby. Rubinstein probably wanted Tchaikovsky to stop neglecting himself and to gain

Nikolai Rubinstein (1835-81), founder of the Moscow Conservatory and gifted conductor.

self-confidence. He even gave him lodgings in his own home for the next five years. Tchaikovsky, however, resented and disliked him at first. Later he changed his mind completely and came to rely on Rubinstein to produce all his musical works.

For the next 10 years Tchaikovsky plunged himself into teaching and composing. It was a difficult and unrewarding period for him. Trying too hard, he put himself under stress and, with important exceptions, few of the works he produced in this period were to stand the test of time. But he was determined to win through. He knew at last what he wanted to do with his life. When a young lady asked him that very question he simply replied "My ideal is to become a good composer."

Young ladies were already becoming something of a problem to him. Vera Davidova, the sister-in-law of his own favorite sister, Sasha, fell in love with him and tried to get him to fall in love with her. He found the whole episode very painful and embarrassing. In 1868 the initiative came from his side, when he suddenly decided that he wanted to marry a visiting Belgian opera singer, Desirée Artot. His admiration for her musical talent was certainly sincere but his other feelings for her may have been born of a wish to find a "cure" for his condition by forcing himself into what others regarded as a "natural" relationship. It came to nothing in the end. Desirée literally went off and married a Spanish baritone while touring Poland — possibly because friends had told her quietly about Tchaikovsky's true nature. Tchaikovsky himself did not appear greatly distressed by the fiasco and perhaps was secretly relieved.

In any case, Tchaikovsky's efforts at composition were causing him quite enough stress, without having to cope with a romance as well. In the summer of 1866 he had his first nervous breakdown. The cause was his first symphony, *Winter Dreams*, which cost him many sleepless nights. And when he made his first public appearance as a conductor, the experience terrified him so much that it was 10 years before he could be persuaded to try again.

In 1868, Tchaikovsky met Mily Balakirev, who had succeeded Anton Rubinstein as head of the Conservatory at St. Petersburg. Balakirev was soon driven out from his post by opponents of his controversial ideas and settled in Moscow, where he suggested to Tchaikovsky that he should compose an overture-fantasy on the theme of Romeo and Juliet. Balakirev not only supplied the basic idea but also sketched the outline of the work and supervised its composition in detail. In gratitude, the young composer

Desirée Artot, a Belgian opera singer with whom Tchaikovsky fell briefly in love.

dedicated it to him. It was poorly received at its première in 1870, but Balakirev suggested revisions which helped to make it, in the end, Tchaikovsky's first great success, and one of his most enduring works.

The composer's progress, however, continued to be uneven. His first attempt at opera, *The Voyevoda*, proved a flop. His symphonic poem, *Fatum*, was bitterly criticized by Balakirev. His second opera, *Undine*, was rejected. He was so distressed that he destroyed the scores of both operas. And his need for money forced him to take up writing musical reviews for the press, an additional chore he much disliked. He should have been encouraged by the warm reception given to his second symphony but decided that it was no good and put it aside until he could make a radical revision of it seven years later.

One of Tchaikovsky's best known works is his first piano concerto, which is full of musical fireworks and has proved irresistible to almost every great piano maestro of the 20th century. On Christmas Eve 1874, Tchaikovsky played it for his friend Nikolai Rubinstein, intending that he should give the piece its first public performance. Tchaikovsky knew that he was himself no more than a competent pianist and wanted the opinion of a real expert. What he got was a verbal battering that left him reeling:

"It appeared that my concerto is worthless, impossible to play, the themes have been used before, are clumsy and awkward beyond possibility of correction; as a composition it is poor. I stole this from here and that from there; there are only two or three pages that can be salvaged, and the rest must be thrown away or changed completely."

"Speechless with amazement and fury," Tchaikovsky declared that he would not change a single note. (Some years later he did make extensive revisions.) Instead he passed the work to the distinguished German pianist Hans von Bülow, who gave the concerto its first public performance at Boston, Massachusetts in October 1875. The American audience went wild and demanded an encore of the entire finale. Rubinstein later changed his attitude entirely and conducted the Moscow première given by Taneyev, Tchaikovsky's favorite pupil.

Tchaikovsky also forgave and forgot. He could disagree strongly without bearing a grudge and when Rubinstein died in 1881, he wrote a beautiful trio for piano, cello and violin as a tribute to him.

The success of the first piano concerto brought Tchaikovsky international fame but little contentment. He had by now acquired the habit of traveling every year to western Europe, driven by a restlessness which made him homesick as soon as he

L BAKST

left Russia and eager to escape again as soon as he returned. "I seek solitude and suffer when I have found it," he noted in his diary. Success scarcely seemed to improve matters "The greater reason I have to be happy the more

Mily Balakirev (1837-1910), leader of "The Five," who both helped Tchaikovsky and criticized him.

discontented I become ... a worm constantly gnaws in secret at my heart."

"Beloved Friend"

In 1876 Tchaikovsky received a letter from Nadezhda Filaretovna von Meck, a wealthy widow who was a great admirer of his music. Over the next 14 years, more than a thousand letters were to pass between them. She became the mainstay of the composer's life, emotionally as well as financially. She imposed only one condition on their friendship — that they should never meet. (In fact they did meet accidentally at least once and turned away from each other in confusion.)

Nadezhda's husband had made a fortune out of the railroads, and his widow, a talented pianist, could afford to patronize gifted young musicians. Madame von Meck began by overpaying Tchaikovsky for routine arrangements of piano works and after 1878 settled on paying him an annual income of 6,000 **roubles**. This enabled him to give up teaching and reviewing and concentrate entirely on composing. He returned the compliment by dedicating his fourth symphony to her.

In 1890, for reasons that are still not clear but may be connected with the death of her eldest son, Madame von Meck suddenly informed Tchaikovsky that she could no longer afford to support him.

The composer was still a very sensitive man, however, and was greatly hurt and confused by this abrupt change, even more so when he found out that she had no money troubles. To his dying day he remained puzzled and wounded by the ending of their friendship.

Nadezhda von Meck (1831-1894), who used her fortune to free the composer from the need to do routine work.

Disaster and Triumph

Despite the fact that he was by now recognized as a leading composer, Tchaikovsky's works continued to be received unevenly by the public and the critics. His prizewinning opera *Vakula the Smith* (1876) fell flat when it was at last performed, and the first production of his now renowned ballet *Swan Lake* in 1877 was nothing less than a theatrical disaster. But by then the composer had something much worse to worry about.

In 1877, Tchaikovsky began work on another opera, *Eugene Onegin*, based on a story by the great poet Pushkin. It tells how a young woman, Tatyana, sends a letter to an older man, confessing her love for him, and is cruelly rejected. Brooding over this tale, Tchaikovsky was astonished to receive just such a letter himself. The writer, Antonina Ivanovna Milyukova, claimed to have been desperately in love with him since she had been a student at the Conservatory. At first the confused composer tried to put her off gently, but he soon panicked when she threatened suicide. Then his aged father joined in, pushing him to take this chance to get married at last.

The marriage took place in July 1877. Two months later the wretched bridegroom was standing chest-deep in the chilling waters of the Moscow river, trying to give himself pneumonia and avoid the disgrace of suicide. He failed to catch even so much as a cold and fled to St. Petersburg, pretending that he had been sent for on music business. There he collapsed, leaving it to his brother, Anatol, to explain to his bride that their marriage was over for good and to pack her off to Odessa at the family's expense.

Very disturbed by this ordeal, Tchaikovsky now set out on years of wandering, convinced that he was either disgraced by the failure of his attempt at marriage or worse

Swan Lake — a poster for a performance at the Bolshoi Theater in 1880.

still, about to be disgraced by revelations of his true nature from "The Serpent" — his ex-wife.

Traveling to Switzerland, France and Italy, Tchaikovsky finished his current symphony and opera, despite the inner anguish which led him to write "I am not happy, not happy, not happy ... happiness does not exist for me." Antonina meanwhile refused to be bought off but, when it was discovered in 1881 that she had had a child, a divorce on the grounds of her infidelity became suddenly straightforward.

Tchaikovsky meanwhile continued to suffer from the varied reception to his works. *Eugene Onegin* was

A dramatic moment from *Swan Lake*, the best-loved of Tchaikovsky's ballets.

not much liked in Moscow but went well in St. Petersburg because the Tsar admired it. His next opera, *The Maid of Orleans*, won deafening applause from the opening night audience but was savaged by the reviewers. His violin concerto, successful in Russia, failed to please in Vienna. And his celebrated *1812 Overture* was dismissed by one critic as "much ado about nothing." Tchaikovsky himself had confessed in a letter to Madame von Meck, written while he was composing the overture, that it "will be very showy and noisy but it will have no artistic merit because I wrote it without love and without warmth." Not surprisingly, given his disturbed state of mind, Tchaikovsky turned down the directorship of the Moscow Conservatory when he was offered it upon the death of his old friend, Rubinstein. Writing to Nadezhda von Meck continued to provide an outlet for the composer's emotions:

"By nature I am a savage. Every new acquaintance, every fresh contact with strangers has been the source of acute moral suffering. Perhaps it springs from a shyness that has become a mania, perhaps from absolute indifference to the society of my fellows, or perhaps the difficulty of saying without effort things about oneself that one really does not think ... in short I do not really know what it is."

Tchaikovsky finally became convinced that all really was well for him at home in 1884 when the new Tsar, Alexander III, saw to it

Alexander III (1845-94) was a repressive ruler, but a great admirer of Tchaikovsky's work.

that his opera *Mazeppa* was produced in both St. Petersburg and Moscow and awarded their composer the Order of St. Vladimir. Reassurance was confirmed by Tchaikovsky's election to the presidency of the Russian Musical Society in Moscow. Assured at last of the respect and regard of his countrymen, Tchaikovsky soon afterward bought a home of his own in Maidanovo, a suburb of Moscow. It was decorated in awful taste and he rarely received visitors. He drank a lot, but in a sense he was at peace. In the following year his *Manfred* symphony, written under the influence of Balakirev, won such

Romantic settings and costumes for a modern English production of *Eugene Onegin*.

universal praise that he was tempted back to the **rostrum** again and in 1887 had the pleasure of conducting a concert which consisted entirely of his own works. The following year, the Tsar marked his approval of the nation's leading composer by awarding him an income of 3,000 roubles a year for life. Deeply respected at home, Tchaikovsky was now poised to begin a new career abroad, not wandering as an exile but hailed as the master musician of his nation.

An American Experience

In 1888 an American music promoter offered Tchaikovsky $25,000 to come and conduct his works in the United States in person. He did not feel free to take up the offer until 1891, and even then it was touch and go when a problem with the nerves in his right hand made him give up conducting altogether for a while.

Shortly after he finally set off, his favorite sister, Sasha, died. Tchaikovsky only learned the sad news when he read about it in a Russian newspaper in Paris. He almost gave up then and there.

The voyage across the Atlantic made him feel even worse, seasick as well as homesick. But the warm welcome he received in America at least distracted him, even if he did still spend hours alone in hotel rooms weeping quietly to himself.

Tchaikovsky's most important task was to conduct four concerts in New York to mark the opening of Carnegie Hall. He therefore met Andrew Carnegie, the generous millionaire in whose honor the concert hall was named. Tchaikovsky also conducted in Baltimore and Philadelphia. Despite a crowded schedule he had time to do some sightseeing and took in Washington and Niagra Falls. And he signed many, many autographs. In a letter he wrote at the time he said he was sure that he was ten times more famous in the United States than in Europe. But then everything in America seemed overwhelming — the hospitality, the applause, the buildings, even the bathtubs! For a shy man it was all rather too much and he was not sorry to depart.

Andrew Carnegie (1835-1919), the poor Scots boy who made a fortune and gave it away.

Triumph and Disaster

In December 1887 Tchaikovsky set out on a European concert tour which also gave him the chance to hear firsthand some of the new music of the day. He began in Germany where he met Brahms. He knew Brahms' music and disliked it — "dry, cold, vague." But he discovered rather to his surprise that he liked Brahms the man very much — "very simple, free from vanity, his humor jovial ..." He was also much taken by the Norwegian Edvard Grieg, who was in Leipzig at the same time. Tchaikovsky then heard for the first time the music of Richard Strauss, which he though "empty" and of Busoni, which he thought "promising." His comment on Verdi's late masterpiece *Otello* was "No comment!" And Wagner simply left him baffled. He recognized an immense talent but could not understand the uses he put it to. After Germany came Prague and then Paris and London — and everywhere warm praise and thunderous applause.

Cheered by this encouragement, Tchaikovsky made 1888 a year of achievement. He moved into a new house and completed the *Hamlet* overture and his fifth symphony. Both works pleased the public but left the critics disappointed, leaving the composer himself downcast. 1889 followed a similar pattern — a concert tour beginning in Germany and ending in London and a productive summer working on his ballet *The Sleeping Beauty*. But when the Tsar saw the gala dress rehearsal in January 1890 he just said it was "very nice." Tchaikovsky was depressed by such faint praise and rushed off abroad, settling in Florence to compose a new opera, based on Pushkin's story *The Queen of Spades*. He returned via Tbilisi in Georgia, where he composed a symphonic poem, *The Voyevode*.

The Queen of Spades was hailed by the public and savaged by the reviewers. Fortunately word came from the palace that, contrary to what Tchaikovsky feared, the Tsar himself had liked it and wanted to commission both a new opera and a new ballet. After an emotional tour of the United States, the composer set to work on these in the summer of 1891. The opera was *Iolanthe*, the ballet was *The Nutcracker*. Once he had completed these he set off on yet another conducting tour, but he became so depressed and homesick that he canceled most of it and went back to Russia. Restless still, he moved into yet another new house in the small town of Klin, then took a cure for his stomach in the French spa town of Vichy, which he hated. Returning home once more, he was depressed by the cool reception given to both the opera and the ballet, then suddenly

A scene from *The Nutcracker*, a lasting favorite with children.

uplifted to learn that his old governess, Fanny Dürbach, was still alive.

The new year saw Tchaikovsky slide deeper and deeper into **melancholy**. He suffered from terrible headaches and found himself weeping uncontrollably for no apparent reason. In mid-February he suddenly began work on a sixth symphony. He finished the first movement in four days and the rest was all mapped out in his head. So he set it aside in May to visit Cambridge, England, where the University awarded him an honorary **doctorate** in a ceremony which also honored his fellow-composers — Bruch, Boito, Grieg and Saint-Saëns.

Tchaikovsky's last symphony — now known as the *Pathetique* — received its première on October 28, 1893. Many people found it rather gloomy. This time the composer was unmoved: "I certainly regard it as quite the best — and especially the most sincere of all my works. I love it as I never loved any of my musical offspring before." Tchaikovsky's last and greatest symphony was born of despair and frustration. Despite the honors and wealth showered upon him, he remained a deeply unhappy man: "I suffer not only from torments which cannot be put into words (there is one place in my symphony where

Tchaikovsky near the end of his life, honored but still restless and unhappy.

they seem to be adequately expressed) but from a dislike of strangers and an indefinable terror — though from what, the devil only knows."

A few days after the first performance of the *Pathetique*, Tchaikovsky complained of stomach pains. The physician diagnosed cholera. It may have come from drinking a glass of unboiled water, or he may have been carrying the germ for some time. Either way, he was dead within four days. That, at least, was the official account given of the demise of Russia's most distinguished composer.

There is, however, a darker story to tell. Recently, Soviet historians have suggested that the glass of water incident may have been a cover-up for a forced suicide. They allege that Tchaikovsky had been discovered having a relationship with the nephew of a duke. Fearing a scandal that would rock society, the authorities had given the composer the option of poisoning himself in return for a cover story that he had died from sudden illness, thus sparing his family from the shame of either scandal or suicide. Scholars still disagree about the real truth of the matter.

When it comes to Tchaikovsky's music there is also disagreement, just as there was when he was alive. It has remained enormously popular with the public which, for a century now, has consistently adored the ballet music, the violin

A century after his death Tchaikovsky's ballets remain as popular as ever.

and piano concertos, the last three symphonies and the delicate *Serenade for Strings*, and even reveled in the **rambunctious** *1812 Overture*. Many of the music experts, however, would endorse Tchaikovsky's own desperate verdict on his work: "I shall go to my grave without having produced anything really perfect in form," although a few days before his death, Tchaikovsky told a friend that he had "a feeling of complete content" on hearing the *Pathetique* symphony. In the words of the Russian composer Igor Stravinsky, one of Tchaikovsky's most ardent admirers, "The point is that he was a creator of melody, an extremely rare and precious gift."

Perhaps, surprisingly, much of Tchaikovsky's work remains unrecorded. A century after his death, therefore, much still remains for music lovers to discover and enjoy.

The *1812 Overture* celebrated the defeat of Napoleon's "Grand Armée" and its attempted invasion of Russia. It has provided orchestras with a spectacular finale item for over a century.

Find out More

Important Books

Tchaikovsky: The Crisis Years by
  David Brown (Norton, 1983)
Tchaikovsky: The Early Years by
  David Brown (Norton, 1979)
Tchaikovsky by Edward Garden
  (J.M. Dent, 1973)
Tchaikovsky: His Life and Times by

Wilson Strutte (Paganiniana,
  1979)
*Tchaikovsky in America: The
  Composer"s Visit in 1891* ed. by
  Elkhonon (Oxford University
  Press, 1987)

Important Addresses

Metropolitan Museum of Art
Fifth Avenue at 82nd Street
New York, New York 10028

Musical Wonder House
18 High Street
Wiscasset, Maine 04578

Shrine to Music Museum
University of South Dakota
414 East Clark Street
Vermillion, South Dakota 57069

Museum of American History
Smithsonian Institute
14th Street and Constitution Avenue N
Washington D.C. 10560

The Music House
73777 U.S. 31 North
Acme, Michigan 49610

Yale University Collection of Musical
  Instruments
15 Hillhouse Avenue
New Haven, Connecticut 72632

Important Dates

1840 Born at Kamsko-Votinsk
1848 Moves to St. Petersburg and
      is separated from Fanny
      Dürbach
1850 Enters School of
      Jurisprudence
1854 Death of Tchaikovsky's
      mother

1859 Enters Ministry of Justice
1862 Enters St. Petersburg
      Conservatory
1864 Composes *The Storm*
      overture
1865 Becomes Professor of
      Harmony at Moscow
      Conservatory

1866	Suffers first nervous breakdown	1880	Composes *Serenade for Strings*
1868	Meets Balakirev; romance with Desirée Artot	1881	Composes piano trio in honor of Nikolai Rubinstein
1869	Writes *Romeo and Juliet*	1884	Decorated with the Order of St. Vladimir
1872	Begins writing music critiques	1885	Writes *Manfred* symphony
1875	Première of the first piano concerto in the United States	1888	First major foreign concert tour; composes fifth symphony
1876	Begins correspondence with Madame von Meck; *Vakula the Smith* performed	1888-1889	Writes *The Sleeping Beauty*
1877	Disastrous marriage to Antonina Miliukov; première of *Swan Lake*	1890	End of friendship with Madame von Meck
		1891	Visits the United States
1878	Receives an annuity from Madame von Meck and gives up teaching	1892	First performance of *The Nutcracker*
1879	Première of *Eugene Onegin*	1893	Receives honorary doctorate in England; composes *Pathetique* symphony; dies

Glossary

Cholera   A deadly water-borne disease, with a high risk of death.

Doctorate   An advanced academic qualification.

Improvise   To play without written music, that is, to make up the music as the player goes along.

Melancholy   A very deep, concentrated bout of depression.

"Romantic" Movement   A period in music, art and literature. In their music, Romantic composers used romantic novels and poems as their subject, expressing extremes of feeling and love of nature among their themes.

Rostrum   A raised platform, on a stage, for a conductor to stand on to lead an orchestra.

Roubles   The Russian unit of currency.

Rambunctious   Boisterous and lively.

Scarlet fever   An infectious illness, once common, that was usually marked by a scarlet rash and sore throat. The illness could cause lasting damage, such as deafness, and was very often fatal to children.

Serf   A servant.

Index

Picture Acknowledgements

The Publishers would like to thank the following for their kind permission to reproduce their photographs in this book:
Catherine Ashmore 25; English National Ballet 22 (photo: Bill Cooper), 28; Mansell Collection 10,11,13,15,23; Mary Evans frontispiece, 6,8,9,12,17,21,26,29; Novosti 18,19,20; Popperfoto 5; Royal College of Music cover.